Interview Questions & Answers

Over 200 questions including variations & answers from the most common through to the tough and the downright insane!

Jules Halliday

Dedicated to

Hollie Graham

For all the times we had in recruitment and a great friendship thereafter.

Introduction

Preparing for a job interview is crucial to your success and while you can't predict exactly what you will be asked, there are techniques you can use to help you second guess the probability of questions likely to be posed to you.

This book contains over 200 questions including variations together with suggested answers and tips to prepare and create your own.

From the most common, general questions through to tough and difficult with some downright insane ones thrown in, you will earn how to maximise your chances at job interviews and stay one step ahead of your competitors.

About the Author

Jules Halliday has over 20 years experience in training, recruitment and management and is Director of TMS Coaching Limited and Founder of www.allukjobsites.com

In addition to writing, she works with individuals and businesses coaching, training and consulting in many aspects of career and personal development.

Out now and available from Amazon, Lulu & Kobo

CV Creator

Interview Strategies for Success

Coming soon…

The Mystery Shopper Series

Contents

CHAPTER 6   **95**

Follow TMS Coaching

www.tmscoaching.co.uk

www.twitter.com/tmscoaching

www.facebook.com/tmscoaching

www.linkedin.com/groups/TMS-Coaching-4561002

Follow Jules Halliday

www.juleshalliday.com

www.twitter.com/juleshalliday

www.juleshalliday.hubpages.com

Follow All UK Jobsites

www.allukjobsites.com

www.twitter.com/allukjobsites

Chapter 1

Icebreakers

Let's start at the very beginning; a very good place to start. Ok, I pinched that from Julie Andrews but the rest of the book is based on experience!

First a quick word on the layout of this book. I have split it into chapters where it has been the most logical way of grouping questions and answers together without driving you crazy with unnecessary repetition. I have started with the most commonly asked question then laid out below variations of the theme. This will allow you to see that although you may be asked many different questions at each interview you attend, in actual fact, many are so similar that you will be able to prepare a base answer and tweak it accordingly. Clever eh?

When you are asked a question at interview think about what the interviewer really wants to hear from you and ultimately why you are the best candidate for the job.

Some questions may seem insignificant but don't drop your guard until the interview is well and truly over. Which leads me nicely onto…

Icebreakers

Or are they?

One of the most common things I hear from my coaching sessions and time as a Recruitment Consultant (and from friends too!) is that candidates were confident that the interview went well as they felt relaxed from the beginning due to building a rapport with the interviewer and found them friendly. In fact, when I ask for feedback prior to the outcome, this is the single most common thing discussed right away.

While sometimes that equalled a successful outcome; more often than not, it set them up for failure in the early stages.

Why? Surely it is great to fit in right away and have some common ground? Not necessarily.

What can be deemed as icebreaker type questions can either be transparent or unfortunately lull you into a false sense of security so unless you are Mystic Meg's protégé or biggest rival then keep your guard up as a precautionary measure.

So, what's the point of this style of questioning?

Well, some interviewers may simply want to put you at ease. If that's the case; all good!

They may just want to buy some time while they are rifling through paper work or gathering their thoughts from the previous candidate, they may not be as prepared as they would like to be so are therefore stalling and breathing (breathing is good!), they may be aiming to build a rapport with you or (and in my experience, most likely) their questions are more loaded than a premier pizza and they have hidden meanings.

Regardless of the agenda, icebreaker questions allow the interviewer to see how you could potentially engage with customers, colleagues and supervisors so what may seem like small talk could actually have a more serious aim.

Really? Yup! Ok; let me give you some examples.

"Tell me about you."

Ok, crikey! What does that mean?

Before you deeply analyse this or any of the following questions, the absolute rule of thumb is keep it professional and relevant to the company or role to which you are applying.

It's acceptable to talk about your career background, your aspirations or what led you to apply for the position but keep it brief. If the interviewer wants to know more then they will ask more questions.

Avoid rambling at all costs and keep your lips sealed even if you are desperate to let the interviewer know that you own four dogs, three cats, a rabbit and two budgies plus a penchant for playing dangerous sports at weekends.

Your prospective future Boss might be an adrenalin seeking animal lover but your shared passions won't necessarily make you the best candidate for the job.

The trick with all interview questions is to plan and practise what you are going to answer to a point where you sound natural and unrehearsed. There's a very high chance that you will be asked about you so at least have something up your sleeve.

The story you tell should demonstrate at least one key behavioural strength that can be transferred to the new role in some way so it's acceptable to talk about anything outside of work that shows strength of character or key qualities and attributes such as integrity, determination, loyalty, working as part of a team and so forth. Just be careful on your decision; being Chief Bridesmaid on a Hen, booze cruise, long weekender may not be the best option to show off your stamina and organisational skills.

Whatever you choose to say; keep it truthful. Don't claim you can bend it like Beckham when in reality you kick a ball like a toddler. You'll be kicking yourself (and be a tad red faced) if your new boss hails you as the next star player in the company 5-a-side team.

If you haven't got a great introduction or are unclear about how to answer; ask the interviewer which aspect of your background they would most like you to talk about.

Avoid falling into the trap of reciting your CV. Not only is this boring but some interviewers find it irritating as they have already read your CV several times in preparation.

Throughout this book there are plenty of questions that have several variations however the answer you give could be the same or tweaked slightly. It's just a matter of trying to decipher what the interviewer actually wants to know and how best to answer in a good quality, professional way.

As an ice breaker, the following is another common question.

"How was your journey?"

"Did you find us easily?"

"How did you get here?"

"Have you travelled far?"

Four different questions there but all the interviewer is really asking is:

"Can you get here on time every day, easily and be reliable?"

You may be wondering why on earth the interviewer doesn't just ask that then. Unfortunately, not everyone feels comfortable being so direct. Strange but true.

Nonetheless, thinking about all the different options and arrangement of questions during your preparation is a good strategy to adopt to minimise being caught off guard. If you can plan for a wide range of questioning then you will feel more in control and confident from the outset.

"How was your weekend?"

"What are you doing this weekend?"

"How do you spend your free time?"

"Tell me about your hobbies and interests."

What is the interviewer really asking?

"Can I rely on you to be here every Monday morning or will you be pulling many sickies?"

Maybe I sound cynical and maybe the interviewer is genuinely interested in your personal life but I doubt it and in any case, your success at interview will be due to your ability to perform the role better than any other candidate and not how interesting your life is.

I said a moment ago, keep it truthful and of course that is a golden rule however it is acceptable to just say "good, thank you" or "I'm just planning a relaxing one" rather than divulging any information that can cause the interviewer to assume your character and ruin your chances of success.

Finally, the interviewer may well be nervous or inexperienced so icebreakers could be more beneficial to them and later in the book we will cover questions the interviewer is not allowed to ask you and how to deal with them!

Chapter 2

About Your Current or Last Role

About Your Current or Last Role

Interviewers will certainly ask you questions about your most recent position and any successes or challenges you had during your tenure.

It's important that you remain upbeat and factual even if you would rather eat a bar of soap than stay there a minute longer. We'll cover reasons for leaving later in the book so for now, some questions surrounding your current or pervious roles.

"What are your responsibilities in your current role?"

"Tell me about what your role involves?"

"What do you do on a typical day?"

"Tell me about your responsibilities at your last job"

You probably already have these on your CV so what the interviewer wants to hear is a more detailed conversation and not just a recital of a bullet pointed list. Aim to connect these to the job you are interviewing for by relating your past or current responsibilities with those in the desirable and essential skills requirements in the job description or person specification.

If your role was varied then try not to waffle and keep your answer succinct to include the transferrable skills and responsibilities. This will allow the interviewer to quickly see you have all the necessary qualifications and experience to do the job.

Avoid dramatizing for effect in case your credentials are checked during the referencing stage.

So, your answer to this question should be a culmination of you researching the current job role and marrying it up to your current or previous positions. Your mantra should be "What do they want? What can I do? What have I done before?"

"What were your expectations for your last role and were they met?"

"Did your last role live up to your expectations?"

Although there's no right or wrong answer to this question, it can be a tricky one so preparation is essential.

Only you know what your expectations were and how the job panned out but it's fair to say that if it was the best job on the planet then the chances are you would still be there (unless you were made redundant or other extenuating circumstances).

It is therefore crucial that you don't slide down the slippery negativity slope while discussing this. Only talk about the role itself and not the company or management. If you can, discuss the most positive aspects of the role, anything you have learned or personal development achievements. Aim to be as specific as you can as this is a chance for you to sell your capabilities and success with the interviewer.

If the role really wasn't what you were expecting then it is fine to say so especially if you have only been there a short time but still focus on being positive and try to find a silver lining to the cloud.

Prepare, prepare, and prepare for this question as it may come in another guise such as:

"What did you like or dislike about your previous job?"

"What was your favourite task in your last position?"

"If you could delegate one task, what would it be?"

"If you were the head of your previous company, what would you change about your role?"

"What will you miss about your previous job?"

"What is something you would want to change about your last job?"

If you liked everything about your last position then that's great but to the interviewer it might seem a bit strange if you are leaving voluntarily.

You need to elaborate and quantify your answer.

"I liked everything about the role however the as it is such a small company, there is no scope for promotion or career development for the foreseeable future and I feel that I can contribute more in this role due to xxxxxxxxxxxx"

The x's are not kisses! Insert here something about the company history, job description or future growth.

"I liked everything about the role however I feel that I will excel in a smaller, more personable environment."

Or

"We had a really strong management team who were friendly and wanted every employee to succeed so I am looking for a role where I can emulate this and encourage others."

If you liked most of your previous role then be sure to talk about the duties that have common ground with the new role. Show the interviewer that you are certain to like this role too and therefore do it well as you already have the experience. The more you research the company and the role, the easier your answer will become.

Don't be afraid to point out what you may feel as the obvious. Link your likes with the current job description.

"One of the things I enjoyed in my previous role was having a detailed knowledge of the products so that I could really listen to the customers' needs and make appropriate suggestions. I notice in this role one of the KPIs is upselling; can you tell me about product training within this company?"

By answering the question in this manner, you have let the interviewer know how fabulous you will be based on your prior experience and also shown an interest in the brand by opening up a two way conversation rather than a question and answer rally.

It can take confidence to do this so if you feel uncomfortable then just use the first part of the answer and incorporate the latter when the interviewer asks if you have any questions.

So what about your dislikes? The interviewer is looking for incompatibilities so once again, ensure you have researched the role fully and steer well clear of saying you didn't like a task that you know is a dead cert in the new job.

Aim to turn what could be a negative into a positive.

"After three years in the role, it became repetitive so I am looking for a more challenging position within a company that can offer me career development."

Or

"The company has gone through major changes in recent times and although I believe change is inevitable, my role has not adapted to these developments."

Or

"I am not keen on cleaning floors but it is an essential part of the role and I feel proud that the customers have a clean environment."

Or

"I like to be the best I can be and would like to have had more on-going training and development."

"What was the most / least rewarding part of your role?"

Not to be confused with likes and dislikes. This question can be a bit trickier to answer as it is vital that you don't include anything that is a major responsibility for the role to which you are interviewing.

Aim to talk about small tasks rather than major duties or just deflect the question if you really didn't find anything unrewarding.

"I didn't find anything unrewarding as even the smallest of tasks contributes to the bigger picture."

Or

"Although I thrive working as part of a team, I didn't always get to see the finished result first hand."

Or

"Certain aspects of customer grievances had to be passed to a Supervisor so although I was informed of the outcome, I prefer to support the customer throughout the process which is why I am applying for this position."

"Tell me about a special contribution you have made to your employer."

"What has been your number one achievement in your current role?"

"What are you most proud of in your current role?"

"How have you saved your employer money and increased income?"

Don't be shy! This is your chance to shine and stand out from the other candidates. It doesn't matter if you have lots of detail on your CV; tell the interviewer how great you are face to face. Let them see your passion and animated explanation.

In my book Interview Strategies For Success, I detail a technique called STAR which interviewers often adopt to gather all the information they need. It's also a good customer service strategy if used in a slightly different way. Here's a brief summary which could help you in this instance.

Situation

Task

Action

Results

You can use this acronym as a memory jogger when talking about your success and achievements so that your answer is to the point.

Situation – What were the circumstances, dilemma or problem that needed solved?

Task – What did you have to do? What were you looking to achieve?

Action – What did you do to be successful? What direction did you take? Be specific here.

Result – What was the outcome? Were there any knock on positive effects as a result of your achievement?

Use STAR to keep the important details to the fore and avoid too much description. It probably doesn't matter what the weather was like that day or what shoes you were wearing.

Or you can use the 3 x Ps.

Get to the P oint, stay on P oint and get your P oint

across.

Don't give long, laborious answers; instead focus your answers on what you did, how you did it and the positive outcomes achieved.

Point taken?

Wherever you can, use numbers for your results.

Result: increased bottom line by 20%

Result: reduced outgoings by £1500 per month

Result: Sold an extra 20 items compared with the previous week.

If you haven't had success that can be numerically detailed then think of other achievements or contributions you made that show you have gone the extra mile for your previous employer.

"In my last job, I organised a team to take part in Race For Life which gave us a great photo opportunity in the local newspaper and free exposure for the company. Not only that, my boss recognised me for boosting team moral."

Or

"I helped train five new recruits on sales techniques and one of them achieved the highest divisional sales the next month. This made me feel very proud and ignited a passion in me to help others succeed."

So, dig down deep into your memory banks and prepare answers where you have contributed to the success or the company no matter how small.

Chapter 3

About Your Boss

About Your Most Recent or Previous Manager/ Boss/ Supervisor

This is where walking on egg shells would be advised. Even if your up line manager or supervisor was the Devil in disguise, always, always avoid negativity, insults or defamatory comments. The person sitting right in front of you will not take kindly to you moaning about your previous boss and the chances are they will presume you may one day talk of them in the same light.

"Who was your best boss and who was the worst?"

"Tell me about your favourite boss"

"I hope will be better than your previous boss. What didn't you like about him/ her?"

Keep this as a positive and respectful answer. If you liked all your previous managers then you are very lucky and if not, then try to think about at least one thing you may have learned from the not so nice ones.

"I've learned from each boss I've had. The good ones have taught me how to be an inspirational leader whereas I have discovered from those I would deem as weaker managers, what not to do."

If you are interviewing in the same town as your previous company or even in the same sector, don't forget that your old boss might actually be a friend or acquaintance of the interviewer!

"What was it like working for your supervisor?"

"What is your opinion of your former boss?"

Although similar to the previous question, you are not being asked directly whether or not you liked you supervisor. I would suggest you keep this answer brief and of course positive. Highlight anything you felt your supervisor did to get the best out of you. Did he or she teach you anything in particular? Would you regard them as a mentor?

"My supervisor was very hands on and was always there to support my colleagues and me."

Or

"He/ she allowed us to work in an autonomous manner but had regular meetings with all employees to monitor their progress."

Or

"My supervisor always ensured that the working environment was fun but professional."

Or

"I have learned a great deal from my supervisor as she was very customer focussed and had an empathetic manner when dealing with complaints."

"Does your boss know you are here today?"

"Have you handed in your notice to your current company?"

"Where are you in the recruitment process?"

Don't worry if you haven't already handed in your notice or informed your current boss of your intentions. Not many people choose to do this prior to securing another role and employers will expect you to have some kind of notice period to fulfil.

The interviewer is trying to establish where you sit within the recruitment process and if you may get a more attractive offer from your current boss to convince you to stay. More on this later.

Just answer honestly. It's not a trick question but if your boss does know that you are planning to leave then let the interviewer know that they are supporting your application or indeed any other reasons such as redundancy.

"What do you expect from a supervisor?"

"Describe your ideal boss."

"What does the perfect manager look like?"

"Tell me about the characteristics and working styles of supervisors you like to work with"

This question is often asked to gauge how you respond to supervision and authority. The interviewer also may try to visualise how you will respond to requests from the current manager and their superiors.

Either way, your answer should be based on what you perceive or have found out about the level of supervision required in the role. You don't want to come across as someone who needs to be micro-managed if the role is mainly autonomous.

Try to strike a balance between someone who is able to work independently yet responds positively to specific instruction.

You may be able to find out more about your new supervisor in advance. Quite often the job description will detail who you will directly report to so you can do a bit of homework in advance.

What is their background? Do they have a Linkedin profile you can research?

Do you know anyone in the company who knows the supervisor and their management style?

Being armed with this information can stand you in good stead. You don't want to be discussing that you like a supervisor who makes the work environment a laugh a minute if the truth is he/ she is a serious task master.

If you really can't find out any information then good general answers would be:

"I am at my most productive when a supervisor has good connections with the rest of the team and is there to support, mentor and guide me to succeed."

Or

"I feel the best supervisors are those who are passionate about the brand, their team and the customers/ clients."

Or

"I appreciate a supervisor who recognises that every member of the team is different, has something to contribute and shows no favouritism."

Or

"I would expect my supervisor to be open and honest with me if there are aspects of the role I can improve upon or do differently with my work. I would also like to feel confident that I can talk to them in confidence if I have any issues relating to my work."

Never under any circumstances criticise a past manager and try to avoid describing your ideal supervisor as super human!

You may like to prepare deeper answers by having some examples of how you have worked well under the supervision of a variety of managerial styles.

"Have you ever had difficulty working with a manager?"

"Tell me about a time when you have had a disagreement with your boss."

"Have you ever had a conflict with a superior at work and if so, how was it resolved?"

"If you know your boss is 100% wrong about something, how would you handle this?"

"If your boss asked you to do something you disagreed with, what would you do?"

If you have then just be very careful with your answer but understand that at some point, most employees have some sort or disagreement or difference of opinion from their manager so it is perfectly acceptable to discuss the situation providing it was resolved and you have learned from the experience.

Differing opinions can in some circumstances be positive if opened up to debate in order to change processes in a positive way for the greater good of the company and its staff.

If you have an example from a long time ago then choose that scenario as your answer. The further into the past the better.

"Early in my career I had a manager who I didn't get along with. We just didn't seem to see eye to eye but now I realise this was a combination of my lack of experience in the workplace and a breakdown in communication. We had different expectations and I felt that by asking questions it was a sign of weakness and inability to do the job.

Now I always ensure that I find common ground with anyone I work with and ask questions immediately if I need clarity on a subject or instruction."

Some interviewers may press on this question as they may find it hard to believe if your whole career relationships have been perfect and without conflict.

"Yes, I have had conflicts in the past but not major ones; more differences of opinion. The way I deal with these is to fully listen and understand the other person's perspective then work together to come up with a solution. I find that if we can identify a common goal then the solution is easier to find."

Buzz words to use in these types of answers are respect, solution, identify, listen, resolve and so forth.

Always ensure that you give brief detail on how any situation was rectified so the interviewer can see you are accountable and don't hold any grudges.

"Would your current boss describe you as the type of person who goes that extra mile?"

"Give me an example of when you have been proactive in a task that wasn't in the job description."

"Would your boss say you are dependable/ flexible/ reliable?"

"Tell me about a time when you have gone over and above the call of duty."

Of course you would like to answer "Yes" to these questions and give examples so how can you elaborate?

Can you think of any compliments you have had from your boss or any clients and customers?

How was your last appraisal? What were the most positive things your boss spoke about?

"I was thanked by the company bosses recently in recognition of me covering extra shifts due to some staff being unable to work due to the heavy snow."

Can you give any examples of when you have been dependable, proactive or even innovative?

What have you done that nobody else has? What did you do first before everyone else copied you?

"What would your current manager say are your strengths?"

"What would your boss say you excel at?"

"What positive feedback did you receive at your last appraisal?"

We often find it hard to tell people what we're good at.

Selling yourself without appearing arrogant is one of the most common interview worries. Many people simply don't sell themselves for fear of seeming big-headed.

Do you know what your strengths are? You'd be surprised how few people do.

One place to start is your recent performance appraisals. What did they highlight as your strengths? Can you supply evidence (provide examples)? Can you relate the strengths to the position you're being interviewed for?

Still stuck for answers to this question?

You could try asking someone. Ask a trusted friend or work colleague. Make sure they give you examples of where you have demonstrated the strengths, so you can quickly use these, if asked.

It's also worth revisiting the job information, to look for which competencies they are looking for. You will make a more favourable impression if you can cover some of these in your answer.

"What would your current manager say are your weaknesses?"

This is not the place to admit your biggest flaws.

It's also not the time to pretend you don't have any development areas – it would make you look either conceited or as though you can't evaluate your own performance.

So how should you handle this type of question?

The main thing is to admit that you have areas to develop, whilst showing that you are already working on them and giving examples of the progress you have made.

If possible, choose a development area that doesn't affect your ability to do the job for which you are being interviewed.

It's usually a good idea to make the "weakness" something small. Avoid topics such as "organisational skills" or "time management"! Be ready to turn it into a positive.

What happens if one of your development areas is one of the key strengths required for the role?

Make sure you can demonstrate why it won't be a problem.

"How do you take direction?"

The interviewer is trying to ascertain whether or not you can be managed and follow instruction without high drama.

Your answer to this question should include that you understand that you should follow instructions from your supervisor and have the confidence to ask questions should you require further clarity.

"Tell me about a time that you didn't work well with a supervisor. What was the outcome and how would you have changed it?"

When you are asked a question that is of multiple parts, break it down into sections and where possible answer in the order in which it was asked.

At some time, most people have had an experience where working with their supervisor wasn't all plain sailing. If you haven't then say so but do try to use an example of either when you haven't worked well with someone in authority in a non-work setting or speak of a time when you noticed a colleague overcome this and what you learned from your observations.

If you have had a time when you didn't work well with a supervisor then be honest however avoid all references to negativity or blame. Answer the question clearly with most of the detail being on the latter part of how you would have changed the outcome. The interviewer is looking for accountability on your part. If you had a rough time then that's ok but it's what you learned and how you will work to avoid a similar situation in the future that counts.

If you have more than one example then it is normally best to either choose the situation where you had a positive outcome or the one earliest in your career.

Chapter 4

Your Work Colleagues

About Your Work Colleagues

"What do your work colleagues think of you?"

"Do you get along with your co-workers?"

"How popular are you at work?"

"Will I encounter any issues with your ability to work with others?"

A fully loaded question, perhaps? This is usually asked to assess your self awareness, integrity and intelligence.

It can be really easy to either fall into the trap of being self-deprecating or the other end of the scale; arrogant. So how do you strike a balance?

The simplest and most effective way of answering this question is to talk of your strengths and how these have in the past related to or contributed to solid, positive team work. Talk to your current or past colleagues and ask them directly. Can they give you any specific examples?

You may prefer to provide an example of how you were the "go to" person such as you have a calming influence on irate customers which could in turn demonstrate that you have excellent communication skills.

Are you a great coach or have good leadership qualities? Can colleagues that you have perhaps supervised or mentored give an example of how you are always ready to listen or help others realise their goals?

Think about your last appraisal. Did your boss mention anything about how well you work with others?

Avoid stating general terms such as hard working or reliable as let's face it; you should display these attributes anyway in any work environment.

Be confident when answering this question. Avoid saying *"I think my colleagues…"* You don't think; you *know*. Once again, be 100% truthful as this question may be asked to referees.

"Tell me about a time when you had to deal with a co-worker who wasn't doing his/her fair share of the work. What did you do and what was the outcome?"

This can be another tricky question to answer as it can be easy to slide down the negativity slope and speak less than highly about a co-worker.

A tip for this one is to find an example when the outcome was positive.

Did you have a co-worker who had personal problems that you didn't know about which affected their performance? If this is the case then how did you find out and what did you do to support and guide them at work?

Did the co-worker appear to be slacking but in actual fact they didn't fully understand the task(s)? How were you involved in ensuring that they received training or coaching and what impact did that have?

"In the staff room, it was often highlighted that James wasn't doing his fair share of unloading the delivery van and he always made excuses to avoid this task by either disappearing to the toilet or taking a phone call. I felt uncomfortable that my colleagues were discussing this without James present and I had a gut feeling that something wasn't right; he wasn't just being lazy.

I scheduled my lunch breaks for the next week to coincide with James' and for the first few, just had general chit chat with him. On the fourth day, James opened up to me that he had injured his shoulder playing football and was frustrated that he couldn't play this season. I quickly realised that this was why he was avoiding doing any heavy lifting at work.

James confessed that he was terrified about losing his job due to his injury because it has happened out of work.

It took some gentle coaxing but later that day, James spoke with our supervisor who worked with him to change the schedule of tasks so that he wouldn't have to lift any heavy objects and replaced this with lighter duties until his injury was healed.

I am pleased to say that James didn't lose his job and his confidence increased so much that he was promoted to team leader later that year."

By giving an answer such as this, you are showing the interviewer that you can look at a situation, remove any assumptions then provide guidance or support to lead to a positive outcome.

If you don't have a real life example of this then you could turn the above into a statement:

"Fortunately I haven't encountered a co-worker not doing their fair share of work but if I did I would try to help. There's a good chance that there is an underlying reason for the lack of contribution so I would avoid any assumptions and aim to listen, support and guide my co-worker to resolve any potential problems."

"Give me an example of a time when you took the time to share a colleagues' or supervisor's achievements with other?"

When have you observed great performance or even the smallest act of kindness in the work place? Did you highlight this and let others know?

Perhaps you were there when one of your colleagues calmed down an irate customer or dealt with a problem professionally and you were so impressed that you shared what you saw?

Did you tell your boss about a colleague who repeatedly does the smallest act of kindness such as opening doors for customers?

It may seem like an insignificant question but demonstrating that you believe that selfless recognition is important in the work place can show strength of character and that you deem team work essential.

"Have you worked with someone you didn't like? If so, how did you handle it?"

I bet you have! Once again it is vital that your answer is professional and avoids running a colleagues' character into the ground.

Admitting you have is absolutely fine and shows honesty so when you speak of this aim to discuss how you found them difficult to like as a person but when you focussed on their skills and how their contribution was valuable to the business, your attitude towards them changed.

You don't have to provide an example of how you became the best of friends and life at work was peachy! It's okay to say that you weren't best buddies outside of work and that your relationship was strictly professional.

"Tell me about a time that you helped someone."

This could be either about someone you work with or a customer. If you are interviewing for your first job then you may also be asked this question in which case you should provide a scenario in your personal life that can demonstrate your future ability to help someone in a work environment.

All the interviewer is trying to assess is your self awareness and compassion.

When describing someone you helped, start with a very brief introduction to the situation followed by what you actually did to help then finish with the positive outcome.

Just like a story; beginning, middle and end. Keep it brief though, you don't want to sound like you are pitching for the Nobel Peace Prize!

"Tell me about a time that you misjudged a person."

This is quite similar to the questions earlier on a co-worker not doing their fair share of work and the one in which you worked with someone you didn't get along with so you may like to tweak your answers and adapt them to fit here. It's unlikely that you will get asked all three questions in the same interview.

Any example you provide should involve your observations, listening skills, action and outcome whether positive or not.

It may be that someone's reputation preceded them but once you actually got to know them you found otherwise.

Most misjudgements happen due to lack of facts or just good old gossip and hearsay so by providing an example the interviewer will quickly establish you are able to be objective rather than subjective.

"How do you get along with older/ younger colleagues?"

Oh! Cringe! This question really shouldn't be asked during an interview as age should be irrelevant and it's teetering on the edge of potential age discrimination but I have chosen to include it as I have been asked this before and have had some of my recruitment candidates in a pickle about it!

Keep your answer brief and positive is the golden rule of thumb and if you can, change the subject quickly or move your answer on a tangent.

You may like to add that in the past you have worked well with older workers and gained additional knowledge from their experience.

For younger workers it's all about their enthusiasm, fresh ideas and energy.

Finish off with you work well with colleagues regardless of their age and that different levels of experience or tenure can contribute effectively to the overall team.

Chapter 5

Your Work Style

Team Player

"Do you prefer working in a team or on your own?"

Think about this one before you answer. This is where knowing the job description and person specification inside out and back to front can provide you with all the clues you need.

Most positions will require you to have flexibility of working styles so aim to give specific examples of how you prefer to both work sole and as part of a team.

Look at the job description and make a list of which tasks or duties may require team work and which will require you to work on your own initiative or in seclusion.

What is the environment like? Is it an open plan office or individual hubs/ rooms? Are you working on the shop floor?

Once you have made your list, ascertain how you can provide brief examples of how you can adapt to both. If you don't have a great deal or detail to work with, aim to provide a general answer.

"In my experience, working as part of a team can get the job done more efficiently, effectively and with great results and differing opinions, skills and contributions can drive business forwards. I do however have the ability to work on my own initiative with minimal supervision and if a deadline is approaching then working solo can increase my ability to concentrate. It really depends on the task in hand and my preference is on whether working as part of a team or working solo will provide the best results."

Tailor your answer to the company needs or the requirement of the role.

Work Ethic

"Do you take work home with you?"

"Do you manage your time in such a way that you complete all tasks before leaving?"

"Will you be clocking off bang on 5pm?"

"If you have multiple assignments that are due at the end of day, but it is not possible to finish them all, what would you do?"

This is a bit of a chicken and egg question and once again, it would be sensible to cover all bases.

If you simply answer "Yes, I do", it may appear that you are unable to prioritise your time, lack time managements skills or have poor communication skills with your boss or team. In your mind you may be super keen and love your work so much that you take it home but this can ring alarm bells with the interviewer that you are inefficient and they may have to pay you overtime not to mention a stressed out, shattered employee.

On the flip side of the coin, you don't want to look like someone who runs for the exit bang on clocking off time.

A simple way to address this is:

"I always ensure that I understand my job role and aim to manage my time effectively so I can complete all tasks on time and with great results. If there are times when additional work or targets and deadlines need to be met then I am happy to take work home with me in order to complete on time."

Show you are flexible and willing without showing that you are incompetent or a mug!

"Do you take pride in your work? How does it show?"

I hope your answer will be "Yes!"

There are many ways in which you can take pride in your work so watch out you don't waffle. Carefully construct a few sentences detailing some of the following which are most relevant to you and the role to which you are being interviewed.

Your appearance and how this in turn can be a representation of the brand.

Do you use the products or service and talk positively about them at all times?

You pay attention to detail so how do you do this? Give a specific example that directly relates to the job.

Think about the place in which you work. Do you have a tidy desk or work space? Even though it may not be your job, do you help keep the work environment clean and free of obstructions?

How do you prepare for your working day? Do you have to visit clients or do presentations? If so then how do you prepare and show how proud you are to work there?

Talk about your organisations skills and work ethic.

Whatever you choose to say, be enthusiastic, positive and naturally animated. The interviewer wants to learn that you can be a great advocate for the brand.

Organisational & Planning

Questions surrounding your organisational skills or ability to plan are typical in job interviews and are designed to discover how autonomous you may work.

Your future boss will be trying to find out whether or not they will have to stand over you and hold your hand while you work.

"How organised are you?"

"What do you deem as good organisational skills?"

"How do you organise your desk?"

"Describe to me how being organised in the work place is important"

"What makes a good organiser?"

When answering any of the above it would be wise to include how being organised can make you more effective or productive at work but try to avoid over used clichés such as *"A tidy desk is a tidy mind"*.

Keep your answer simple. You don't have to describe how you have invented a new filing system that is going to change the world. All the interviewer wants to hear is that you understand how important it is to be organised so you are not wasting time trying to find hidden items or working in chaos.

"How do you plan a typical work day?"

"How does planning effectively positively impact your day?"

"How do you prioritise and plan your appointments?"

Giving an overview of your planning strategy is recommended rather than a step by step account of every hour of your day.

"I start my planning the previous day by ensuring that I have everything organised, neat and tidy before I leave at the end of my shift. This allows me to start the day knowing exactly what I have to do and where I have to be."

Or

"I always aim to manage my time in the most effective way so when I am booking appointments I try to

arrange them in blocks of postal areas so that I am minimising my travelling time and reducing mileage costs for the company."

Or

"My day starts with a short team meeting so we are all clear on our agenda and if any cover is required due to staff absences. This allows us to prioritise the most urgent tasks and delegate as required in order to achieve all tasks."

"What environments allow you to be especially effective?"

"How do you like your work space to be?"

"What atmosphere do you prefer to work in?"

Questions such as these are often posed to ascertain your flexibility to adapt to different work place environments or settings so your answer should address this.

"Over the course of my career, I have worked in a variety of settings and have learned to adapt to differing environments. To be at my most effective depends on the task in hand. For example, if I am working to a deadline where the task requires high concentration, I am more effective in a quiet place where there is minimal interruption however I realise that this is not always possible so I have learned over time to be able to block out excess noise and focus solely on my work."

This answer allows you to cover several bases without laying out a diva-ish list of requirements.

Another angle is to think about the environment you will actually be working in should you get the job.

If you know you are going to be working in a fast paced, open plan office where noise will be inevitable then avoid stating that you like to work on your own in silence. Ensure your answer in this instance takes into account the potential to be interrupted or distracted and how you would go about making sure you deliver a high standard of work at all times.

"I am able to work in a variety of situations but I am especially effective when there is a fast paced environment with energy from others radiating around the office."

Similarly, if you will be working alone for most of the day then this needs to be discussed.

Chapter 6

Role & Research

Role & Research

"What do you know about Our Company?"

A typical job interview question, asked to find out how much company research you have conducted is "What do you know about this company?"

It is absolutely essential that you do your research. I know many interviewers who have ended the interview immediately if the candidate does not know a great deal. In fact, I personally have done this several times when the answer has been "Not much" or limited in response. This may sound cruel but investing time in someone who hasn't taken the time to at the very least find out the company history just does not make good business sense.

This and the following question are designed to screen out candidates who aren't serious about the position or who are applying for a stop gap until something better or more suitable comes along.

You can find out an abundance of information from the company website if they have one (the about us section is a great place to start), advertisements or stories in the press, television and even product packaging.

Research the company history; when was it founded and by whom?

What is their mission statement, values and culture?

How has the company developed and what plans do they have for expansion and development in the future?

Who is the big boss? Are there any other managers or directors?

Have they won any awards?

Do they offer training programs?

Any charity work or commitment to the local community?

What are the opening times?

If you have visited the company as a customer, what was your experience like? Have you called them? If so, how was your call handled.

Taking the time to research can only ensure that you make a good impression with how much you know about the company and shows that you are making an informed decision with your application.

"How did you find out about this job?"

This is not meant as a trick question so there is no need to prepare a detailed answer. Interviewers normally ask this just for marketing purposes.

"Why Do You Want To Work For Us?"

It's rare for an interview not to include this question and the great thing is that if you have researched the company, you already have the information to give a great quality answer.

Most interviewers want to hear that their prospective future employees are enthusiastic about the company and its products or services so based on your research; this is your opportunity to give a clear indication on why you would be a perfect fit for the organisation and its people.

Combining your research and the previous question on what you know about the company, you can then demonstrate that you fully understand the company's position in the market place, your commercial awareness and that it is the actual company you want to work for and not just the job title. By all means relate the position and opportunity to your desire to work there but make sure you show that it is them you want to work and not any of their competitors.

Ensure your answer is sincere and you actually believe it! There's no point in gushing about how amazing the company is and how honoured you would be to work there if deep down you couldn't care less and just need a job to pay the bills. Interviewers can see through smoke screens.

It is important to base your answer only on how you are the right candidate for the job so be sure to avoid stating that you want to work for them because of the salary, benefits, working hours or that it's across the road from your home! Those may be some of your reasons but it's best to keep schtum for now.

"Why should we give you this job?"

"Why should I hire you?"

Are you ready to blow your own trumpet? This is your chance to pitch for your life and excite the interviewer with your USP (Unique Selling Point); your attributes that make you different and in effect better than any other candidate.

Most candidates I speak with find this question uncomfortable and some embarrassed as they feel like they are begging. I understand that fully so think of this; If there were two equally qualified and experienced candidates for the job and you are one of them, what would you say to make sure you were the one to get hired?

There's a fabulous phrase used in business called the 30 second elevator speech which is often used when pitching products or services. Networking meetings often use this format so that everyone in the room talks about their business or service for 30 seconds and therefore everyone gets an equal chance to introduce what they do to the others and in turn hopefully strike up some great conversations and future relationships.

Speed dating also uses this formula and even finalists in TV reality shows do the 30 second "Why you should vote for me" speech.

Reminding yourself that although this question may seem alien to you or uncomfortable and that it is quite common in other environments can help to increase your confidence at promoting yourself so you will feel less like you are begging.

Practise, practise, practise this one.

What can you say in 30 seconds in a compelling way that will add interest and uniqueness to you above all the other candidates? In my book CV Creator, I suggest presenting your personal statement and cover letters as though they were a movie trailer; would you buy you?

Think of the interviewer as the buyer. What do they want? Be prepared to listen and look for buying signals throughout the interview. If he or she is nodding, smiling or agreeing to particular aspects of your previous answers then this is a good indication that they are "buying in" to what you are saying so refer back in some way to these skills or statements. Of course you can't necessarily prepare for this in advance so use these buying signals to compliment your prepared answer.

To prepare effectively, the key is to highlight your strengths and prior experience in relation to the job role and how these will benefit the company in both the short and longer term. You are the product so think about what the buyer (the company/ interviewer) needs.

Remove words such as hard working, reliable, nice, good timekeeper and so forth as these should be a given anyway and do not make you unique.

Show you are passionate, have the experience and knowledge together with an absolute tenacious desire to succeed. You have the skill and you have the will.

Don't forget to smile! Rabbit stuck in headlights is never a good look!

"What interests you about this job?"

This is very similar to "Why do you want to work here" so it's time to make a list again. Use an A4 sheet of paper and divide it into two columns.

Grab the job description, person specification and all the research you have done on the company and make a list in one column of all the key qualities, skills, experience and qualifications that are essential and desirable in the role. In the second column write a list of everything you have (or just use ticks next to the items in column one) and then cross reference them.

In short, write down what they want and what you have.

Use this list to establish everything you have (albeit small) that matches the requirements of the company and let the interviewer know that not only do you possess all these key skills and attributes but based on your research of the company you can then describe how these relate to the role and company culture.

What interests you about this job = your skills match and synergy with the company values.

In all cases, you will want to convey your enthusiasm for the opportunity to interview, along with your solid ability to do the job.

"What are you looking for in your next job? What is important to you?"

Once again, a good old place to start is the job description, why you have chosen to apply for that particular company and your reasons for leaving your last role.

This is another question to work backwards. What is important to you? Is it career progression? If so then you should have researched what the promotion structure looks like within the organisation.

Maybe you are looking for stability for your family life. That's fine to mention however avoid going in to too much detail as employers should not ask any questions relating to your marital status, children or personal life if unrelated to the role.

"What challenges are you looking for in this position?"

"I notice from the job description that I will have to meet monthly sales targets so I am looking forwards to the challenges that will bring. I am motivated to succeed and always aim to exceed any targets set."

Or

"In my previous role I spent most of my working week in the office on my own so embracing the challenge of working as part of a face to face team excites me."

Or

"I realise that a new superstore is opening locally which will be in direct competition so I am looking forward to the challenge of ensuring the highest standards of customer service at all times to retain the current customer base and work to increase this by positive word of mouth."

You may also choose to ask the interviewer which challenges you may be expected to face in the role then add that you would be able to deal with this due to the experience you have already gained in similar circumstances.

The interviewer will be looking for solutions not a face of shock so watch your expression here.

They will ultimately be looking to see that you are motivated and excited by challenges so your answer should be upbeat and if you can provide any examples of how you have overcome challenges in the past then now is the time to voice them.

Chapter 7

Accountability

Accountability

"Tell me about a mistake you made at work."

"What have you learned from your mistakes?"

"Tell me about a problem that you solved in a unique way"

It's unlikely that an interviewer is expecting Mary Poppins so don't worry if you're not practically perfect in every way. What they will be expecting is for you to demonstrate your accountability; how you dealt with any mistakes or errors of judgement.

If you are asked these types of questions then the name of the game is to give examples of how you turned a negative into a positive. If there was a solution; there was no problem.

A bigger problem would be to say that you haven't made any mistakes. You probably have but just either haven't realised or don't care to admit it.

All men make mistakes but only wise men learn from their mistakes.

Winston Churchill

It's absolutely fine to admit that you have made mistakes in the work place. Keep the examples brief and generalist. Now is not the time to tell of the time you left the washroom taps running and flooded the ground floor or of when you turned up with a hangover and spent all morning being sick!

"Early in my career I felt that I had to know everything about all of the products and sometimes gave incorrect information. This on a couple of occasions led to customers returning products or complaining. My lack of experience made me feel that I would be showing incompetence if I could not provide any answer but fortunately my supervisor was supportive and helped me to realise that it is acceptable to refer any questions to someone in the team who is more expert or has more experience than me. This way the customers receive a better service."

Or

"I think one of the most important things I've learned is persistence. Not to give up too soon, because the solution is probably right in front of me. I used to get frustrated and feel like I had failed but over time this has turned into determination."

Or

"I am always enthusiastic about my work and find it difficult to say no. I have learned overtime that I don't have to say yes to everything and I have to weigh up quantity over quality of workload before reaching a decision."

Whatever you choose to say for this one it is essential that you are honest and show that you have learned and moved forwards.

"How Did You Handle Challenges In Your Previous Role?"

When asked this question try to be as specific as possible without divulging any information that may be confidential, compromise security or reveal anything sensitive about your previous organisation.

Discuss how you (and team if applicable) researched potential solutions before a final decision was made.

Did you implement any operational procedures that increased productivity or contributed to the smooth running of the company?

Talking in monetary or numerical terms will always help here.

Remember S.T.A.R? What was the situation? What did you have to do? (Task) What action did you take? What was the result?

Strengths/ Weaknesses

"What are your strengths and weaknesses?"

Oh here we go! Of all the people I come into contact with, this has to be the one that stumps everyone and there seems to be a 50:50 split on whether they find it easier to talk about their strengths or their weaknesses.

It's a hugely popular question with interviews so careful, considered answers with examples are a must.

Whether you are asked about your strengths, weaknesses or both it is essential that they have relevance to the role. There's no point in talking about how fabulous your communication skills are if you will be required to work on your own never coming into contact with customers or colleagues. If however you are interviewing for a customer facing or telephone role then stating that you are an excellent communicator who can build rapport easily with a variety of people would be a simple way to highlight your strength.

Really analyse the role. What key characteristics are required? What tasks will you be performing on a day to day basis? If you are applying for an analytical role that requires number crunching then stating that your weakness is maths is not going to do you any favours.

Think about what the interviewer wants to hear and of course avoid what you think they don't want to hear. Keep in mind that each answer you give should add value to the position or company.

There are many variations of strength and weakness questions including:

There are variations of strength and weakness questions:

"Are there any areas of your work that you could be more effective in?"

"What work skills do you think you can improve on?"

"What would your previous employer say your weaknesses are?"

"What is the one key attribute you possess that helps you excel in the workplace?"

"What qualities were highlighted positively in your last appraisal?

They are just variations on the theme so prepare your answers for your strengths and weaknesses then adapt accordingly.

So let's take a look at your strengths.

"What is your greatest strength?"

Whatever you state here, make sure you can back it up with an example. There's a high chance that if your answers revolve around management or team leading skills you will be asked later in the interview to provide examples on how you have successfully managed a team. You don't want your credibility to take a nose dive if you can't answer.

If you talk about a quality such as paying attention to detail for example, you may be asked to elaborate on how that will help you perform in the role.

Avoid all the over used clichés and meaningless phrases such as team player, hard-working, patient, positive, reliable, good time keeper unless you can quantify your answer with tangible results or scenarios.

Go back to the job description and person specification again and analyse what you think you would expect the greatest strengths of the person in the role should be. Do you possess any of these qualities? If you do then that's where you should start. If the documents state that a requirement is creativity then if you can demonstrate how your creativity translates to the role then fantastic!

Perhaps working to KPI's (Key Performance Indicators) is listed. If that's the case and you have achieved or exceeded targets in the past then now would be a great time to highlight this as a strength.

"One of my strengths is that I am motivated to achieve and exceed set targets. In my last role I was successful in hitting all sales targets and improved by 5% on prior year."

The interviewer may follow this up with a question such as:

"Describe to me the action you take to ensure you achieve these targets."

Your answer could *be "Another of my strengths is my ability to take the bigger picture and break it down into small manageable tasks. I look at the target I have to achieve, say by the end of the quarter and then work out what I need to achieve on a daily, weekly and monthly basis. By doing this I can strive to be the best I can be on each day."*

Providing examples such as these which are directly related to the job give the interviewer another opportunity to visualise you in the role.

"My greatest strength is my ability to focus on my work. I'm not easily distracted, and this means that my performance is very high, even in a busy office like this one."

What real life examples can you think of? Perhaps you are a dab hand at dealing with customer complaints with patience, empathy and objectivity.

When faced with a challenge or a problem do you have the ability to remain calm, focussed and positive?

Are you a superstar when it comes to planning and preparation?

"My organisational skills are my greatest strength and together with being able to prioritise and plan effectively I'm capable of keeping many projects on track at the same time ensuring deadlines are met."

If you really can't think of anything then take the time to ask a colleague or your supervisor. I am sure they can.

"What is your biggest weakness?"

Now don't go running yourself into the ground with this one.

Often I hear that you should choose a strength and portray it as a weakness. I can see why some people would choose to adopt this route but in all honesty, interviewers are savvy to this approach and may not take kindly to being deceived.

A better approach is to admit that you have a weakness and talk about how you recognise this and are working on it or have taken steps to fully overcome it. This shows more strength of character that the preceding paragraph.

Try to keep it simple especially if you suffer from nerves.

One of the best examples I encountered was a candidate that told me she gets frustrated when colleagues don't share her work ethic and grab any opportunity to skive off (her words!) or pull a sickie. She then explained that she has now learned to bide her time as these people always get found out in the end.

This then led into me asking about what their working relationship was like when they did show up for work. Her answer was simple;

"I always strive to have a good working relationship with all my colleagues regardless of their ethics or morals. We all need to work together to get the job done and be as productive as possible while the opportunity is there."

These were really basic, simplistic answers but gave me exactly what I wanted to hear. What she deemed as a weakness was actually a strength to me as she had the ability to make the best out of a bad situation.

You may be thinking that I should have followed up this with a question on why she didn't tell her supervisor that her colleagues were slacking off. Well, firstly I don't like interrogation questions and secondly (I had already asked several questions by this point) I felt that this showed a respect for her supervisor as she did say that they always get found out in the end. I was more interested in the fact that she kept her cool, her patience and remained focussed on the job.

Whatever you choose, you must show that you have or are at least trying to change this. By recognising that you have a weakness and are working to change or reduce this is another example of your self awareness and accountability.

"When faced with a project I sometimes find it difficult to get started as I generally have lots of creative ideas. The way I try to overcome this is to start with the end in mind. Once I have established what the result has to be I can then list all the important points to get there. When I have the order ready, I can then tackle the beginning and my creative flair can be added along the way."

Or

"When I know I am getting close to closing the deal, I tend to get excited and talk too quickly and at too high a volume. I know this is because I am passionate about the product and enthusiastic about the sale but to customers it can feel like they are being rushed. I researched calming techniques on the internet and although there were many helpful tips, I found that he best one for me is slowing my breathing and relaxing my shoulders which really helps slow down my speech and reduces the volume. I have noticed a significant increase in my cross and upselling success since doing this."

Or

"In the past I have found planning and prioritising a challenge. I now use Outlook on both my computer and work mobile phone to sync appointments and block out time for travel and the unexpected. I find this much easier than using a handwritten diary as I can now move tasks and appointments around should I have a cancellation and see at a glance what is coming up."

What you don't want to say is that you find it hard to start projects as you are a daydreamer, you let everyone in the room hear you are about to seal the deal or that your desk looks like an explosion in a paper factory. Make yourself sound appealing, not appalling.

Steer well clear of stating you are a perfectionist, you work too hard or you are too flexible. Statements such as these are difficult to substantiate and could well come back to haunt you in the future.

Back to S.T.A.R again. Situation, Task, Action, Result.

Our strength grows out of our weaknesses

Ralph Waldo Emerson

"What would you say has been your greatest failure?"

This is fairly similar to discussing your weaknesses in that it would be sensible here to discuss a particular failure of a task with the inclusion of what steps you took to overcome it.

Think about a specific example in the work place if you can but only if you have learned from the failure and that you certainly won't fail in the same way again. What exactly did you do and did you seek any advice?

If you are a graduate or interviewing for your first job then aim to keep it related to education or a hobby.

"Give me an example of a situation where you didn't meet your goals or objectives."

It's okay to describe a situation where you didn't meet expectations providing you show what steps you have taken since then to avoid a similar failure. If you have been absolutely brilliant and achieved all goals and objectives in your career then give an example of when things nearly went wrong and how you managed to turn it around. This is much better that saying that you don't have an example because you have been great all of the time.

Once again, where possible, relate the situation to the role to which you are interviewing but if you really can't then think a skill which may be transferrable from outside the work place.

"In my last role I didn't achieve my sales targets for the first quarter of the year. I always over achieved my

targets as January is the month where we historically have the highest sales and due to this past success I assumed this year would be the same. I normally break down my targets into weekly goals so I know exactly what I have to work towards and this time I didn't. I have learned my lesson and now ensure I always plan in advance and never assume. On a positive note, I did make up the difference in the second quarter."

Avoid situations where you may have under achieved because you were on holiday or ill. The interviewer will wonder why you didn't have the foresight to talk with your supervisor or put plans into place to counteract the effect of your absence.

Chapter 8

Your Credentials

&

Characteristics

Your Credentials

"Are you overqualified for this job?"

This is a fairly common question that can halt someone's confidence mid-flow but is mainly asked to establish if you are going to take this job then leave when something better or more relevant to your experience comes along.

"I prefer to think of myself as fully qualified instead. Yes, I have worked at a higher level than this position in the past however this job and company offer the exact career path that I am looking to take. I believe that having additional experience to what is required will be an asset to you in both the short and longer term."

It may well be that you are looking for a lower level role due to some down shifting in your life such as spending more time with your family or looking to work closer to home. If this is the case, be completely honest. Any employer will value someone with higher credentials if the honesty and integrity is well placed. They will be getting more for their money, after all!

"How has your education prepared you for your career?"

This is a common question asked to candidates interviewing for their first job and can appear like a broad question so take great care to avoid waffle and a lengthy answer.

Focus on how your education has prepared you by including how well you have worked with others as part of a team and also the dedication you displayed in order to achieve your qualifications.

Aim to keep your answer relative to the role. If you are interviewing for a position in a shop then talk about how interacting with your fellow students has taught you valuable lessons about customer service or engaging with others.

Did you lead any class projects or have any roles of responsibility such as a Prefect, Peer Mentor, Head Girl/ Boy? Perhaps you collaborated with others on organising or running the school fete.

Try to use behavioural examples where you can rather than solely talking about academic achievements.

When talking about your academic achievements or qualifications don't assume that the interviewer knows exactly what you are talking about. They may not have taken these qualifications or if they did, it may have been a long time ago so although you should keep your answers brief, try to include detail so everyone can understand. This is especially important if you are at a panel interview.

Avoid jargon, acronyms or abbreviations for the same reason.

Sometimes an interviewer can ask a seemingly simple question which may not appear to be challenging but combined with the other questions they can add to the bigger picture of your credibility, honesty and sincerity.

"How are your computer skills? What programs and software are you familiar with?"

This should easy to answer and the interviewer is just looking for a list of programs you are familiar with and not an in depth discussion on what each one does.

If you are learning a new technical skill then now would be a great time to let them know.

"Do you try to learn something every day?"

This doesn't mean that the interviewer is expecting you to be studying for a degree in your spare time; it's more about self-awareness and continued professional development.

"I always learn something new at work whether that is how to improve my communication skills or deal with a new situation."

Or

"I try to keep up to date with industry trends and developments by reading publications and both local and national news articles."

"How would you describe yourself in three words?"

Quite simply use strong words such as organised, intelligent, loyal, dependable, honest, sincere, determined, competitive, resourceful, innovative, and creative and such like.

Do be prepared for follow up questions though in which you may be required to back up these words.

"Talk to me about a time when you have showed determination"

"What have you done in your recent past that shows creativity?"

"Give me an example of your resourcefulness"

If you claim it; be prepared to explain it.

"On a scale of 1 to 10 how happy are you?"

This is not exactly the most inspiring or delving question on the planet but it is often asked nonetheless.

Just keep it simple and go for a 8-9. Anything less may lead to the assumption that you are down in the dumps or may bring personal issues into work. A 10 might not be believable.

Chapter 9

Behavioural Questions

Behavioural Questions

Behavioural questions are designed to uncover how you handle certain situations; how you do or would behave.

Hypothetical questions can also be used to establish your character or behavioural traits such as "What would you do if…" "How would you react if…" In other words; real answers for imaginary situations.

Interviewers use both styles of questioning to find out not only how you have behaved or dealt with situations in the past but as a predictor of how likely you will act in the future.

"What annoys you?"

"What makes you angry"

"How do you react when you are angry"

The interviewer is most likely to be asking this to find out if you are a good fit for the company or team but go steady; you don't want to sound like an old moaner or look like you will lose your cool at the drop of a hat!

Choose something fairly insignificant for this but keep it related to work. Saying that you hate it when someone talks loudly on the phone or your blood boils when customers want a refund is unlikely to gain you any points.

Play it down. It is acceptable to say that you are not keen when someone is consistently late for work without good reason but you understand that it is your supervisor's responsibility to address this issue and you don't let it affect your work.

Maybe you are a manager? In this instance you may choose to talk about a situation that you have to deal with such having to reprimand one of your staff. If this is the case then make sure you include that although it annoys you, you know exactly how to deal with it.

"When was the last time you were angry and what happened?"

The interviewer is looking to see how you will deal with challenging situations and if you have the ability to stay calm and professional. You may have read this standard answer before (I have heard it many times while interviewing!) but it is so good I could not omit it.

"Anger to me means loss of control. I do not lose control. When I get stressed, I step back, take a deep breath, thoughtfully think through the situation and then begin to formulate a plan of action."

"How persuasive are you?"

"Show me how convincing you are"

"Give me an example of when you have changed someone's mind"

Don't worry! This question does not mean you have to start begging! It is really about your abilities to lead, coerce or direct.

Think of a time when you had to build trust with your co-workers in order to convince them to do a task.

What did you have to do? How did you go about it? What was the outcome? Use this as a template for your beginning, middle and end.

Did you have a team meeting or was success down to having individual conversations?

"How do you react when you receive "No" for an answer?"

Avoid here any answers that may suggest you never take no for an answer or that you react badly.

"I understand that sometimes my ideas may be rejected but in that instance I always ask for feedback so I can take it on board and improve next time."

"Define good manners? What kind of people do you think deserve to be treated with good manners?"

"Good manners is being courteous at all times and remembering not only the basics such as please and thank you but acknowledging how a colleague or customer may be feeling. I believe that everyone deserves to be treated with good manners and respect regardless of the situation."

"How would you handle a client from another country?"

"In the same way as any other customer however I may have to slow my speech if there are language barriers and I would respect and adapt to any cultural differences."

"Tell me about a time when you stood up for something you believed in"

Try to relate this to your passion and belief behind an idea or product in a work related setting and the positive outcome your standing your ground had. Avoid anything political, religious or personal.

"Tell me about a time when your work was criticised. How did you handle the situation?"

"How do you respond to negative feedback?"

The interviewer is trying to establish how you will react to feedback and if you will use any negative comments to move forwards and improve.

You could relate your answer to a former appraisal and show the improvement you made by the time your next one came around.

Allow the interviewer to see that you understand that criticism can be a positive step towards improvement and success.

Dealing with challenges, pressure and stress

"Can you work under pressure?"

This is a closed question so it can be tempting to answer with "Yes", "No" or "Sometimes" but what does that tell the interviewer? Not much and it may leave you open to more probing questions. All the interviewer is looking to establish is your ability to cope in stressful situations or perhaps meet challenging deadlines.

"Yes, I can work under pressure however I always ensure I plan in advance as much as possible which I find reduces the chance of me feeling pressured considerably."

Or

"Yes, in fact in my previous role I often had to work to short deadlines so I always made sure I was organised and planned for these dates accordingly."

Or

"Yes. I am very target driven and the pressure to achieve and exceed company expectations is an area in which I thrive."

I hope you notice that I haven't given you an answer for "No" or "Sometimes".

Answers to stress or pressure related questions must be practised as much as possible prior to the interview. If you are an absolute bag of nerves when answering, you won't look sincere!

"Give me an example of a situation where you faced conflict or difficult communication problems"

"Tell me about a time when you had to deal with a conflict at work"

"How do you deal with conflict?"

Companies on the whole look to hire employees who can calmly deal with a multiple of situations calmly and without or at the very least; minimal conflict.

When asked this question, avoid at all costs belittling anyone you have previously worked with and keep your answer factual and to the point.

Use one example only! You don't want to look like you have had lots of arguments or disagreements in the past which may mean that you will be a fire cracker in the new work place.

If you have dealt with conflict in the past, now is the time to highlight how you can rise above conflict, take control of the situation and diffuse any heated emotions in a mature, calm way.

If you don't have a specific example where you were the hero of the hour, try to think of a situation where you worked with others to rectify the problem to demonstrate your team working and communication skills.

As always, a work based example is best but I am sure that if you don't have a real life professional answer then you will have come up against conflict or communication problems in your personal life. If you choose something personal then think first of the environment in which it occurred. A drunken, pub Saturday night story is probably not the best to highlight your expertise in conflict management!

"What do you find are the most difficult decisions to make?"

"What was the most difficult decision you have made in the last year?"

"Tell me about a time when you had to make a difficult decision without all the information you needed"

"When was the last time you took a risk and how did it turn out?"

When choosing your answer here, the trick is to show the interviewer that you don't shy away from making difficult decisions and you are prepared to take calculated risks.

You may be interviewing for a more senior position than your previous role so in that case you could give a hypothetical answer.

"Although I have not had to directly terminate anyone's contract, I would imagine that would be a difficult decision to make. In that situation I would ensure that I had taken the appropriate steps in following company procedure and protocol to performance manage the member of staff so that the final decision would be easier to make."

Or

"I believe difficult decisions are the ones where you have limited information of the facts so if faced with such a challenge it is important to conduct further research."

"What is the most difficult situation you have faced?"

"Define difficult"

Similar to the above questions however this time the interviewer is trying to decipher what you deem as difficult. Are you on the same wavelength? Are you pessimistic and get stressed at the slightest of challenges?

Think of a difficult situation you have faced and then detail how you overcame it.

Motivation

"What motivates you?"

If you've got that you're a highly motivated person on your CV, you need to read my CV Creator book to find out why you should remove it.

The answer to this question can only be based on your past experiences so choose something that will help the interviewer to understand what makes you tick in a way that shows you will do well at and enjoy the role.

Whatever you choose to answer, make sure that it is honest, sincere and you have the facts to back it up. What do you actually enjoy while at work? Did you have an experience where you got that buzzy feeling of excitement? What's the one task that you love doing because you know you do it well; what motivates you to keep doing it well?

"Knowing that I am going to do a great job motivates me as I want to be successful."

Or

"Exceeding sales targets and in turn increasing my commission has always been a driving factor in motivating me to be the best sales person I can be."

Or

"Ensuring that each and every customer is happy motivates me so that each year customer retention is increased."

"Are you self- motivated?"

This question differs in that the interviewer is asking if you are able to be motivated to work with enthusiasm with either limited or no instruction.

"Yes, I enjoy my work and I always look for ways to set myself challenges or bring new ideas to the table."

"What drives you to achieve your objectives?"

In other words "If I set you a new task or challenge, can I feel confident that you will be committed and get the job done?"

"Knowing that I have a challenge and can get it done on time and with great results drives me to succeed. I take pride in my work and want to be the very best I can be."

Chapter 10

Comparisons

Comparisons

Comparison questions are a gift as they are your chance to really sell yourself by telling the interviewer why they should choose you above all the other candidates. We have already covered "Why should I hire you" earlier in the book so here are more similar questions however this time you the interviewer wants to weigh you up against all the other potential candidates. Comparison questions are without a doubt decision making questions and if you are asked these then there is a high probability that you are doing well!

"What new skills or ideas do you bring to the job that our internal candidates don't offer?"

Internal candidates can often be your biggest competitor as many employers look upon sideways moves or promotions as more seamless and cost effective. No matter how amazing an external hire is; it still takes commitment, money and time to train and induct the new employee. Internal candidates can therefore be viewed as less of a risk.

Now is your chance to invite the interviewer to visualise how your external commercial experience can benefit the company and even if the internal candidate has more qualifications or hands on experience, you can add more value particularly if you have worked for one of their competitors or have transferrable skills which the other candidate may not have.

Back to the job description, company research and commercial awareness again. What can you bring from the outside and action immediately? Can you see any gaps in the role or weaknesses within the company that you can use your expertise to positively change these?

Be bold! What can you offer that they can't?

"We're considering two other candidates for this position. Why should we hire you rather than someone else?"

Two, five, ten…the number is irrelevant here so only focus on why we should hire you.

If you are asked this towards the end of the interview, use the information you have gained during your conversation and stress any points where you have seen positive buying signals from the interviewer. It's the same question as "Why should I hire you" and you know how to answer that one already.

Chapter 11

Your Future and Loyalty

Your Future/ Loyalty

Questions surrounding your future and loyalty to the company are becoming more and more common in interviews. Gone are the days where you collected your carriage clock in your 60's for forty odd years' service at the same company. People move onwards and upwards; employment is more transient than it has ever been so the interviewer needs to know if it is worth investing time, money and energy in to you or if you will be off with a hop, step and a jump as soon as a better offer becomes available.

"What are your aspirations beyond this job?"

"Talk to me about your career progression plan"

"Once in this role, what would be your next step?"

We'll come to "Where do you see yourself in five years time?" in a second. The questions above are more immediate and can be answered only by knowing the promotional and departmental structure within the organisation is laid out.

You may already have found out some of this information in your initial research but it is always worth asking the interviewer to give you an overview of what career progression may look like and cater your ambitions around their answer.

All the interviewer is looking for is your commitment and passion to succeed together with what value you can add in the future.

It is important to let them know that you are a good investment and while your focus will absolutely be on the position you are interviewing for, you also have the desire to develop and move onwards and upwards.

"Where do you see yourself in 3 / 5/ 10 years time?"

"What are your goals for the next five years?"

"What is your dream job?"

"What are your goals in this job?"

So onto the old classic and an almost guaranteed question. Let's start with what not to say.

Gone are the days where "I want your job" or "I want to be running the company" or even worse "I want to be your boss" are acceptable answers.

Ambition is one thing but being cocky is another. Even if you do actually believe that one day you will be running the company; you need to structure your answer around what benefits you will bring to the company in the long term and you are fiercely loyal and determined to succeed without alienating the rest of your co-workers along the way.

"I want to be the best I can be"

"I want to get promoted"

"I want to be in a more senior role"

Avoid these answers like the plague. They are vague and scream "me, me, me". Show you are serious about your career and you are committed to the organisational success while understanding the company's structure, vision, culture and mission.

Try not to state specific job roles but instead talk about leading, managing or increased responsibility and the action you would take in the offered role in order to get there such new experiences or training and development.

In my experience, the most successful answers come from developing a two way conversation with the interviewer showing interest in the corporate structure.

"Why do you think this industry would sustain your interest in the long haul?"

This is another way of asking *"What excites you about this role/ industry"* or *"How passionate are you about your chosen career?"*

"This industry is always moving forwards and changing. I enjoy the challenge this brings and how it is essential to keep up with advancements. It excites me that in some way I am a part of the changing face of the industry."

Or

"I believe in the company products and the benefit they bring to the customer. I notice that this company uses customer feedback to develop the product range and that is what attracts me to work here long term."

"What will you do if you don't get this position?"

Even if you are only joking, please don't reply "I'll cry". I can't even remember the amount of times a candidate has said this to me. No blubbering wrecks, please!

"If I don't get this position I will ask for feedback and take that as an opportunity to correct whatever stopped me from being successful so that I can apply in the future. Is there anything at this stage that is preventing me from being the strongest candidate?"

Bold maybe but you have nothing to lose. By asking the question at the end of your answer, you may have the opportunity to influence their decision before you leave the room and it certainly shows assertiveness.

Avoid stating that you will be disappointed but you have more interviews lined up so you're bound to get something or that you will apply to one of their competitors.

Asking how you will feel if you don't get the position is more commonly asked if you are applying for an internal promotion so the interviewer can either establish if it is just the progression you are interested in or how they may have to manage your disappointment. Will you leave if you don't get the promotion or will your current work or confidence suffer?

If you are interviewing for an internal promotion then aim to reassure the interviewer that you are committed to the company and once again you will take on feedback to establish what you need to do should the opportunity represent itself. Let them know that you are the best candidate for the job though!

"How do you plan to achieve your career goals?"

"How do you plan to further develop your career?"

It's all very well saying that you would like to progress up the career ladder but how are you going to get there? There are not many companies who promote solely based on longevity of service.

Does the company offer in-house training or are there any courses you plan to attend in your spare time? Are you a member of any professional organisations which offer CPD (continued professional development) or are you an avid reader of career and personal development books?

Do you attend business conferences, presentations or master-classes?

Really think about what you want to do and how you plan to get there to give your answer more substance. It doesn't have to be specific; in fact, far from it. You want to be able to demonstrate your flexibility and not a tenacious desire to follow out your carefully constructed plan to the letter.

"What would you do if one of our competitors offered you a position?"

This is where your answer should be based on why you want to work for this company.

"This is the company I feel I have the greatest synergy with and can offer the most value. I already use your products and believe in the brand so I will be sincere in my sales approach."

You've already researched the company, role and person specification so you know that they stand head and shoulders above their competitors, right?

"What would you do if your current boss offered you a pay rise to stay?"

This question was an old favourite of mine when I was a Recruitment Consultant to establish how serious a candidate was about leaving their current company. Often I would be informed that they would stay!

It begs the question "Why haven't you asked for a pay rise?"

Are you leaving your job because of the salary? If a raise isn't possible then you may feel compelled to tell the interviewer this but in my experience it signals alarm bells that you are only wishing to change roles due to the money and nothing else.

Remember earlier the question "Why do you want to work for us?" and use this as ammunition to make it clear your reasons for the job change and how it relates to your career progression or ambition rather than the dosh.

"Which other companies have you applied to?"

Another of my recruitment favourites and an interesting one for interviewers. Be very careful that you don't trip yourself up if you have already answered questions stating that you don't want to work for their competitors yet then say that you have applied to them!

It can work in your favour though if you have applied to other companies if you are a strong candidate as it could speed up an offer letter as they may press you to accept before you attend an interview anywhere else and it could also help you in your salary negotiations if they know you have more than one offer on the table.

Avoid saying that you have applied for loads of companies and can't remember all the names as this will certainly look like you are not serious about the position on offer and are desperate for any job.

"What is the highest level job you expect to hold in your career?"

This is simply to find out how career focussed or ambitious you are and once again can give the interviewer an idea of how loyal you will be to them.

If you say that you aspire to a position the company will not be able to potentially offer in the future then this may reduce your chances of securing the role unless it is in the far away future so they will retain you for a long time.

Chapter 12

Customer Related

Customer or Service Focussed

"Tell me about a time when you had to deal with an irate customer. How did you handle the situation?"

"Can you give me an example of a particularly difficult customer you had to deal with and how you used your skills to successfully overcome the problem they had?"

Remember the questions surrounding dealing with conflict? This one is in a similar vein. The interviewer is looking for evidence that you can keep calm, be diplomatic and methodical in your approach to work with the customer to find a solution.

Your answer should include an example of when you have diffused a situation in a professional manner.

The key points you are looking to include are that you:

Listened

Thank the customer for bringing the issue to your attention

De-personalised the situation

Repeated the customer issue back to them in your own words to confirm that you have understood

Remained calm

Spoke slowly and of a low volume

Apologised (if this is appropriate)

Empathised

Took responsibility of the situation

Took action

Worked with the customer to find a solution that they were happy with or sought help from a more senior member of staff

Confirmed that they are happy

Thanked the customer before leaving.

If you haven't had a great deal of experience with direct customer contact or telephone resolutions then either choose a time where you followed company procedure and referred the customer to your supervisor but be sure to include what you would do if you had to deal with such a scenario in the future.

If you haven't had any experience whatsoever, you could spin the answer around so that you talk about a time when you were the customer and how your problem was resolved. What did you learn from the process and how would you use that in a work place setting?

"What have you done to promote great customer service?"

"What does great customer service look like?

"How to you ensure that customers have a great experience?"

So what does great customer service look like to you? What do you like as a customer?

If during your research for the company you either called or attended as a customer then using your findings as a base for your answer would show that you have a good understanding on how their customers are treated.

Where possible, try to find a past example where you went the extra mile for a customer or implemented a new idea or procedure.

Have you ever had a thank you letter or email from a customer or has your previous boss complimented you in some way?

"What are the key factors which make a successful call centre?"

This is where your research comes in handy especially of you haven't worked in such an environment as this is a common question to find out if you have an idea of what to expect by way of the work atmosphere. Thankfully most interviews at a call centre start with a tour round the building so you will get a sneaky peek at the room first.

Construct your sentences around:

High energy

Enthusiastic and motivated employees

Targets

Team work

Leadership

Excellent customer service skills

Politeness

Articulate conversations

Positive attitude.

Chapter 13

Managing & Team Leading

Managerial/ Team Leading

Most interviewers will be keen to hear of your management style. Do you dangle the carrot or whip with a stick? They are looking to establish whether or not you will fit in with the existing team and quickly build trust and respect so really do prepare your answers in advance and find out as much about the company culture and values as soon as you can.

Just like the behavioural questions earlier in the book, the management or team leading questions will usually take the format of competency based and hypothetical questions; Tell me about a time when, give me an example of and what would you do if…so having clear answers to include real life situations will be expected.

The interviewer will be expecting to hear that you manage effectively and lead by example so words you should include within your answers are:

Fair

Honest

Considered

Methodical

Supportive

Mentor/ coach

Listen

Motivate

Inspire

Lead

Develop

Performance

Not all within the same answer though!

"Give me an example of how you have dealt with an under-performing team member in the past."

"What was the situation?"

"How did you deal with it?"

"What was the outcome?"

The interviewer is most likely looking for an answer which shows that you have taken appropriate steps to assess the situation based solely on facts and what action you took to improve it.

"In my last role I had a team member who was underperforming so after analysing his figures I had a one to one conversation with him where I listened to how he felt his performance was. We quickly established that he had lost some of his confidence and needed some support. We then worked together to create a plan of training and development and evaluated his progress on a weekly basis until he was up to speed."

"How do you motivate your team in challenging circumstances?"

Be careful here that you are not only providing answers that may be based on incentives or treats. Show that you have good leadership skills and your team members are motivated to get the job done as they value you and want to be successful rather than you having to only bribe them.

How do you communicate with your team when faced with a challenge? Do you give clear instruction and plenty of verbal recognition to spur them on? Do you recognise that each member of the team is an individual so therefore may need differing levels of support and guidance or appropriate tasks assigned to them depending on their level of competency?

"Describe a situation in which you inspired trust and respect in your team."

As you are interviewing for a new role then a great example would be when you started your last managerial job and got your team "on side".

"When I began my previous role my team had been without a steady manager for over a year and had three temporary ones so I had to gain their trust and reassure them that I wasn't going to be there for a short time then leave. I implemented a team huddle meeting at the start of each day which lasted 15 minutes with a "anything can be said inside these four walls policy". Having this regular face to face contact time with the team helped us get to know each other quickly, nip any problems or worries in the bud and work as a collective to find solutions. Within a month the meeting evolved into more of an ideas session where everyone had a voice and could share their creativity with each other. I found that my team's confidence and morale soared and their productivity

increased continually by over 10% each month thereafter."

Notice with this answer that there is nothing to say "I got them to trust me" or "I inspired them". The example demonstrates how you were the guide who steered them on the path to success and didn't just simply tell them what to do.

"What kind of manager are you?"

"How would you describe your team leading abilities?"

"How do you take charge of your team?"

"What are the most important qualities of a supervisor?"

"How do you lead a team?"

"What management style do you find most effective?"

Your answer should include how you encourage your team to get the job done and not a blow by blow account of your day to day duties as a manager.

Points to include would be:

Working together as a team

Approachable

Diplomatic

Tactful

Motivating

Knowledgeable

Adaptable

Supportive

"I believe that working as a team of which I am one of the members is the most effective strategy to adopt as we are all working to achieve the same end result. I find that I don't use only one management style as I

have to adapt according to the individual needs of the team members. This may mean that newer or less experienced staff may require more instruction and close supervision whereas higher performing or more experiences workers may be able to work more autonomously or be set more challenges to keep stimulated and motivated.

Regardless of their level of competency, I always ensure I provide support and encouragement together with recognising their achievements and sharing this with the rest of the team which builds confidence and inspires others."

You may like to talk about how you are able to exert your authority in certain circumstances or that you have great coaching or mentoring skills. Be sure to provide examples.

"What would you change about your management style?"

This is just another was of asking "What is your greatest weakness" but making it more specific to the role so whatever you answer, use the same rules as before.

"How have you handled having to give someone difficult feedback?"

Choose a scenario where the feedback was difficult to hear rather than you finding it difficult to dish out. Allow the interviewer to see that feedback is important to you and your team and although it may be difficult to hear, it is the only way to either improve or performance manage effectively.

Managing Change

"What is the first thing you would change, if you were to start work here?"

Your answer to this depends on how much you know about the job however tread with caution so as to avoid saying anything that may be deemed derogatory to the current or former post holder.

Why has this position become available? You should be able to find out this information I advance. If not; be bold and ask the interviewer. I am quite sure they aren't expecting you to be telepathic.

Before you start, consider setting the scene by saying that your first priority would be to establish the boundaries of responsibility, the team in which you will be working, what kind of changes you would be permitted to make and who would be your next line authority figure to sign off any proposals. This is a much better strategy to adopt than simply stating "I would do this or that" unless of course it is clearly stated that the role is predominantly to make a fast, aggressive changes.

Talk about how you would consider the impact any changes may have on the direct team and wider work force with empathy and that any changes would have to add value to the organisation both in the short and longer term

If in doubt, ask the interviewer what the weaker areas that can be improved upon are and use that as a base for your answer.

"How do you manage change?"

"How do you deal with change?"

"Are you able to work in a fast paced environment?"

Change in the workplace is inevitable especially in these tough economic times so you may either be interviewing for a role in which you will be managing change or be involved directly in dealing with changes.

Most of the time, change can be difficult for others to deal with so being able to lead a team or colleagues through to the other side and giving examples of your success can lead to respect and reassurance that you are calm, collected and positive.

Regardless of the superiority of the role, having an example or two to demonstrate how you cope with or lead change will put the interviewers mind at ease. If the organisation is developing or moving in a different way that previously then it is unlikely that you will be aware of all the facts prior to or during your interview as the interviewer may have to keep certain points strictly confidential.

What they are looking to see is that you accept that change is inevitable, you embrace it and you will be unfazed by any challenges or complications along the way.

Always talk positively when referring to another company and be very careful that you don't divulge any sensitive information. It is acceptable to talk loosely about the facts and the interviewer will appreciate this, after all they need to know that you aren't going to tell all and sundry private matters about them.

Give a brief synopsis on what brought about the change, your direct involvement, any positive impact this had together with any challenges and how you worked to overcome them.

"Tell me about a time when you felt that a planned change was inappropriate"

Only provide an answer to this if you can openly talk without compromising confidentiality or sensitive data. If you are able to answer then choose a situation where you successfully challenged the proposal. Keep your answer upbeat and professional omitting any personal grievances.

"Give me an example of a change you initiated and what positive outcome it had"

Rather than launching into an example here, aim to set the scene by discussing how you go about your roll out plan step by step.

Have you had to initiate redundancies for the greater good of the company future?

Did you change the structure of your team? If so what were the outcomes. Did save money or increase productivity?

"Give me an example of when your team were reluctant to change and how you overcame this"

I bet you have lots of examples here!

The main points to consider are the relationship you have with your team and how you listened to their concerns before reassuring them.

Most interviewers will want to hear that you recognise that not everyone is comfortable with change but you can lead and guide them through the process as a result of trust you have previously gained with them.

Chapter 14

Difficult or Personal

Difficult/ Personal

First off, there are certain questions that an interviewer is not supposed to ask however many do so let's cover these first.

Interviewers should abide by the UK discrimination laws and avoid any questions which may put them in breach of this yet you may be sitting in front of an inexperienced interviewer who unwittingly asks banned questions as they think they are either being friendly or attempting to break the ice.

As a potential employee, you are protected by other legislation including the Sex Discrimination Act, the Race Relations Act, the Employment Equality Regulations and the Disability Discrimination Act.

Let's take a look at what an interviewer should not ask and later solutions on how to deal with them.

Questions about Place of Birth, Ethnicity and Religion

Acceptable questions are any surrounding your ability to provide original documents proving your right to work in the UK, any visas, your passport and birth certificate for example. It could be deemed discriminatory if you are asked where you were born or if you have an unusual surname; it's origin.

You may have been asked to fill out a form during the application process on your ethnic background. This is fine as this information is used for monitoring purposes and the data capture is usually anonymous and should not be brought up in the interview. You should have had the option to choose this or decline to answer.

If the position requires someone who is multi-lingual, the interviewer should ask which languages you speak as opposed to what is your mother tongue.

An interviewer should not ask any questions regarding your religion. They may however ask if you are able to work on particular days (which may or may not be a religious festival) if this is directly related to you performing the role.

Questions about Your Age or Gender

Since October 2006 it has been illegal to discriminate against workers under the age of 65 on the grounds of age however there are some instances where you may be asked to provide your age if it is what is called a "Genuine occupational qualification."

Minimum age restrictions apply to those working in licensed premises such as serving alcohol or working in a betting shop, the armed forces and police; young workers are not permitted to come into contact with chemical agents, toxic material or radiation.

In these circumstances, the interviewer should not ask your age outright and instead ask questions such as "Are you over 18″ or are you above the minimum age required for this role?"

Similarly, you should not be expected to answer questions relating to your retirement.

Regarding your gender; you should be considered for the role based on your ability to perform and prior experience. You may be the only female in what is a male dominated company but being asked "How do you feel about managing men?" or "Could cope being the only female in the office?" is unacceptable.

Questions about Marital Status, Children and Sexual Preference

This seems to be the area in which interviewers do ask questions to make polite conversation however they are not permitted to do so. By all means volunteer the information yourself as part of your conversation if you really must but do any of the above make you a better candidate for the job? Probably not.

You may be asked if you have had any former names as part of background checks or referencing but asking outright if you are married and/ or have children is irrelevant.

According to Which? the most commonly asked banned question is about whether someone is thinking about starting a family. It says this kind of enquiry is simply unacceptable. The consumer group argues firms should be focusing on a person's knowledge and skills and not making pre-conceived judgments about their age or other personal circumstances.

As for sexual preference. No! It's completely unrelated to your performance in the role.

Questions about Disability and Illness

It's perfectly acceptable for an interviewer to ask for an explanation on number of sick days you took at your previous work place for example and don't panic if you are asked "How are you?"!!!

Questions that are off limits are whether you are currently taking medication, if you have had any past illnesses or operations or if you have taken time off work due to stress. Any questions posed to you should be framed as "Are you able to perform the specific duties for this position?"

Rethink.org advises "The Equality Act 2010 has restricted the questions that a prospective employer can ask about health or disability in an application form therefore you do not normally have to provide information about your health on your initial application. An employer may still ask these questions but they should only be asked for specific reasons eg. To enable the employer to make reasonable adjustments in the interview or to establish that an applicant can carry out tasks necessary for the job."

If you disclose that you have a disability, health condition or mental illness as you know it will interfere with the job you are applying for then you will be protected by the Equality Act 2012 (EqA) which means that it will be illegal for the prospective company to discriminate against you. Ensure that during the interview you are able to discuss your skills, experience and qualifications that make you a strong candidate.

If you do have a condition or illness you feel you should disclose, you can do this at any time either before the interview, during the interview, after the interview but before a job offer, after a job offer but before starting a job or any time after starting a job. Only you know whether or not it will affect your day to day duties.

Questions about Your Lifestyle Choices

You may have your hobbies and interests listed on your CV and an interviewer may ask you more on this which is fine however lifestyle choices such as alcohol consumption, smoking and drugs are not allowed.

Asking if you are a member of any professional organisations or bodies that are related to the position is acceptable. Requiring an answer to if you are a member of any clubs or societies is not.

You may be required to take a CRB check (Criminal Records Bureau) for the role which could be completed before the interview however no questions surrounding the results and detail may be asked and regardless of any checks no questions relating to arrests or convictions.

Your height and weight are other areas in which you should not be asked although if the role requires you to lift items to a high level or heavy weights then you may be asked if you are capable of doing so.

How to answer inappropriate interview questions

Interviewers cannot ascertain your ability to do the job based on your age, sex, religion, gender, marital status and so forth so you are not compelled to answer.

If a question makes you feel uncomfortable then you can choose either to briefly answer and change the subject quickly (a good way to do this is to ask the interviewer a question that is directly related to the role or the company), ignore the question altogether and move on or politely decline to answer. If you move on quickly to another subject area the interviewer may realise their mistake and appreciate your deflection and skill to let it go and move forwards.

If however the question is clearly discriminatory or offensive then you have every right to end the interview and leave. Ok, so you may not get the job but would you really want to work there anyway?

Remember though that the interviewer may ask questions innocently due to lack of experience or indeed their own nerves (yes, interviewers do feel nervous too) so assess the situation before you hot foot it to a legal representative!

Exceptions

Of course as with most things, there are exceptions to the rule.

Theatrical professions are just one example of the employer permitted to move the goal posts. If an acting role commands a particular ethnicity, gender or age then they can choose to only audition those who fulfil the criterion.

Slimming and wellness organisations may weigh you or ask questions surrounding your health and wellbeing.

So the general rule of thumb is that if it the question is not directly related to the job then an interviewer should not ask you to answer it.

Difficult Questions

So what about difficult questions? Well the key here is to try not to panic and definitely avoid saying "I don't know" as this can imply that you don't have the ability to solve problems. An incorrect answer is actually better than nothing at all. At least you had a go.

Take your time to consider your answer; the time passing won't be as long as you think. When you are nervous or put on the spot five seconds can seem like an eternity to you but it won't to the interviewer so take your time.

If the question has multiple parts to it, break it down and answer each section step by step.

So what are difficult questions? Well that is difficult to answer! They are any questions that may cause you to sweat under the collar or those that you don't have a prepared answer for. While you can second guess most of the questions you are likely to be asked during the interview based on the job description, person specification and research you have conducted on the company, there will of course be questions that take you by surprise.

If you feel the question is over complicated or unclear then ask the interviewer to repeat the question or rephrase it. You may be sitting in front of an inexperienced interviewer who is not trying to catch you out and not purposely making the questions difficult or vague. They just don't have the eloquence that many others have in this situation.

Reasons For Leaving

"Why did you leave your last job"

"Why are you leaving your job?"

"Why are you looking for a career change?"

This tends to be deemed as difficult to answer yet you have a high probability of being asked this.

Always, always avoid negativity even if you were fired (which we will come to in a minute) and demonstrate good reasons for your decision to move on while highlighting anything positive you gained from the position such as experience, learning, training and development.

Points to avoid:

You hated your boss

You hated your colleagues

Nobody liked you

The job was overwhelming

It was too stressful

You were over worked and under paid

Of course if these are your real reasons for leaving, I am not suggesting you lie and make up a fake answer! Focus on a positive aspect of the job then relate it to the organisation you are being interviewed for.

"I really enjoy working with people and my previous role was mainly solitary. I know that working here will give me the opportunity to use my skills in providing great customer service while working as part of a team"

Perhaps you are leaving because the daily commute is a complete nightmare and you can't bear it any longer to be standing on a crowded train with a sweaty arm pit in your face? That's okay to use that as a reason but your answer should include that you really want to work for that particular company too and it's not all about the convenience. Employers tend to favour workers who are closer to the company as a reduction in travelling time can lower potential levels of stress.

"While I enjoyed my last role, the daily commute was lengthy so I am looking to work closer to home as I feel this will make me more productive. I chose to apply to your company because...."

Or

"I was commuting and spending an hour each day on travel. I would prefer to be closer to home so I have been looking for a local company that is a good fit for my skills and experience."

Ensure that you can answer that the company and job description is a perfect match for your skills and experience. Lucky them that you want to work closer to home!

Another answer would be that you are looking for more responsibility or a greater challenge. Refer back to the section on why they should hire you and why you want to work for them and adapt your answer accordingly.

"My last position wasn't a great fit and I decided it made sense to resign and to refocus my career path."

You may have been working part time or studying and now you are looking for a full time career.

"I graduated from university/ college/ left school and resigned in order to find a position where I could use my education and related experience."

Or

"I resigned because the position was part-time and my personal situation has changed so I need full-time employment."

If you were fired from your last job, then you should come clean as there is a huge chance that your previous employer will be asked to provide a reference.

Reasons for leaving – You were fired

First off, once again refrain from any negative comments and use the opportunity to stress that you have learned from the experience. Keep your answer as brief as possible. An interviewer does not want to hear the nitty gritty of "She did this; he said that; it was so unfair". Never, ever play the victim. You were fired for a reason so step up and take responsibility and show that you have learned from the experience, have changed and are a better person as a result.

Suppose you were fired because you were continually late for work. Here you should explain that you struggled with time management skills and what you have now done to rectify the situation.

Reasons for leaving – Redundancy

"The company was cutting back and, unfortunately, my job was one of those eliminated"

This should be a sufficient explanation. Redundancies are more and more common these days and should not be a reflection of your capabilities. It was the role that was made redundant; not you.

Gaps in Your Employment

"What have you been doing since your last job?"

"Why have you been out of work for so long?"

If you have gaps in your employment history, you are almost certainly going to be asked questions as to why. Aim to have these gaps addressed on your CV so that you are not caught on the hop with tricky or uncomfortable questions when face to face. It doesn't matter what you did so long as you can fill the gaps in some way.

Be honest but let the interviewer know that you have been proactive in some way rather than them assuming you have been a slave to day time TV.

In these tough economic climes, it is more and more common to interview candidates who have significant or several gaps in their career history whether that has been through choice or not so try not to worry that this will hamper your chances. It is very unlikely to have a negative effect as long as you can show some kind of positive activity. They did invite you to the interview after all!

If you have taken time off work to raise a family or study then this should be easy enough to explain and detail on your CV.

If you have been unemployed involuntary then it is crucial that you talk about what you have been doing during this time. Don't just say that you have been applying for lots of jobs as this may make you look like you are desperate for any old job (even if you are, hide the fact) so instead allow the interviewer to see that you have had time to think about which jobs match your skills and you are more passionate than ever that this is the right career path for you.

Have you attended any training courses? Maybe you have been researching careers online or read a number of career related or personal development books?

If you have completed any voluntary work then now is the time to talk about this and any additional skills you have gained.

"What has been the biggest disappointment in your life?"

"What is your biggest regret? Is there anything that can be done about it?"

Although interviewers should refrain from asking personal questions, bizarrely this is a common one and it is designed to see how you cope with disappointment. Deflection is probably best here.

"I haven't had any major disappointments. Any adversity I encounter, I try to remain positive, learn from it and look on the bright side"

Or you may like to choose something unrelated to work that is not too personal or a complete disaster.

"My wife and I had our hearts set on our dream house locally and when it came up for sale we immediately made an offer. Unfortunately we were outbid but I am sure that we can find another equally perfect house if we keep looking."

Salary

"Tell me about your salary expectations"

"Tell me what you are worth"

"On a sliding scale from £-£, tell me where you fit in"

"What package are you looking for?"

Everyone wants to earn a decent salary and at the very least; what they are worth.

Before you answer any questions surrounding salary expectations, it is advisable to research your sector and if you can, find out the salary range the company is willing to offer together with any benefits that may be added or included.

By having the knowledge of what salary is likely to be realistic, you will be in a stronger position to negotiate a reasonable package.

If you have no way of finding our prior to the interview the salary range on offer then ask the interviewer and place yourself on the scale accordingly in line with your experience and sector average.

Most employers will expect you to answer any questions surrounding your compensation history so beware asking for £50,000 per annum if you have never earned above £30,000.

Never, ever exaggerate your earnings as this may be checked at the referencing stages and if you have not been truthful about how much you have earned previously it could throw your credibility into doubt.

Take the time to remind the interviewer how you match the criteria, skills, qualifications and experience listed in the job description and any other details that would make you an asset to the company above all other competing candidates.

Negotiating your Salary

This is where you have to think carefully and absolutely prepare in advance hot only what you want but also what you need.

Money is not the only thing on offer in many jobs so find out what the benefits are. Many companies offer a selection of the following:

Pension

Travel expenses

Company car

Discounted or free meals

Uniform

Gym membership

Health or life insurance

Medical care

Enhanced holidays

Flexi-time

Free training

Bonuses

Incentive rewards

Professional memberships

Whatever is on offer remember that everything can have the potential to be negotiated so talk in terms of the whole package and not just the money but in order to be effective, you need to have all the facts.

Don't feel pressurised to give a complete answer at this stage. You haven't got the job yet and the last thing you want to do is alienate yourself from the running.

Politely give a salary range or indication of the package and say that you will give this your full and informed consideration if you are offered the role.

Most interviewers are just looking for a rough idea to see if they are able to afford you but if you are pressed for an answer then go for the mid-range so that you have room for negotiations when the offer is on the table.

Be confident and clear rather than ambiguous and nervous.

Never mention salary in an interview unless you are asked. The same goes for holidays.

Sean Wadsworth CEO of Nigel Frank International recommends:

"One of the most tricky interview questions to answer can be around the package you are looking for. In my experience provided a candidate can do the job and is a cultural fit for the organisation then the answer to this question is usually the only stumbling block to receiving a job offer.

In the heat of the interview resist the temptation to embellish the truth or sell yourself short as ultimately you risk pricing yourself out of the job or getting an offer that you don't want to accept.

If asked the question my recommendation would be to be as flexible as possible. Explain what your current package is including all benefits and state whether you would be looking for a progression on that. If you are looking for a progression be prepared to back it up with a logical reason -not just "I think I'm worth it"

If you have submitted a desired salary on an application make sure your answer is consistent with that.

Unless questioned on salary it is not a topic I would recommend a candidate brings up in an interview."

Chapter 15

Insane or Weird

Weird and wonderful interview questions

So either the interviewer has a specific reason for asking crazy questions or they have lost the plot. I will leave that up to you to decide.

Mostly these questions are asked to find out about your personality, creativity, self-awareness or how you would solve problems. Personally I think they are a bit "Blind Date" but if they are good enough for Cilla Black then they are good enough to include in this book!

When answering any of these questions, try to relax. It's okay to smile or chuckle a bit but don't collapse with belly aching laughter or shriek in shock. Take time to think of your answer although there may not be a definitive right or wrong.

"If you were an animal, what would you be?"

This is predominately to assess your personality. Think of it in the same way as "How would your friends describe you?" Try to choose an animal that is strong, loyal, confident or with other clear cut personalities that would be related to your perceived performance in the work place.

Dog, lion, tiger, elephant maybe but fluffy bunny rabbits or slippery snakes are probably best avoided.

Whatever you choose you should give a reason for your answer and link it to a quality that the interviewer is looking for but make sure that your choice really does fit with your personality. There's no point in saying you are strong as an Ox if you are more like a wall flower.

The interviewer tends to use these questions as a wild card to see how you can think on your feet and react to unique scenarios. This will in turn allow them to see whether you will be a good fit for the company, as well as how creative you are.

Similar questions include:

"If you were a biscuit/ drink/ colour/ tree, what would you be?"

"If you could have any super power what would you choose?"

"If you could be any cartoon/ film/ TV character, who would you be and why?"

"Who do you most admire?"

"Who would be your ultimate dinner party guests; dead or alive?"

"What's your favourite colour and why?"

"If you could be a cocktail, what would you be?"

Then there are situational questions which are similar to the hypothetical style of questioning we covered earlier and are designed to find out how self-confident you are.

"You arrive at a party and you are the only one in fancy dress; what do you do?"

"You are at a business lunch and your meal is under cooked. How do you react?

To find out a bit more about your personality and character:

"What's the last book you read?"

"What is the last film you saw at the cinema?"

"If someone wrote a book about your life, what would the title be?"

Questions to establish whether you are creative, logical or lateral in your thinking:

"Why are your legs longer than your arms?"

"Why are wheels round?"

"How would you describe a car to an alien?"

"What colour is your brain?"

For goal setting, ambition and planning:

"If you had only six months to live, how would you spend your time?"

"If you won a million on the lottery, how would you spend the money?

You may also be asked to answer a riddle or puzzle so good luck with that!

Chapter 16

Questions to Ask the Interviewer

"Do you have any questions?"

You can pretty much bet your life that you will be asked this towards the end of the interview.

Almost all interviewers on the planet will ask "Do you have any questions?" so always have several prepared. Asking just one or two questions is adequate but always have at least four or five at the ready as some may already have been answered as part of the conversation.

Good questions are:

How many people are in the team and how is it structured?

How will my performance be measured?

Can you describe to me a typical day in the job?

How would you describe the responsibilities of the position?

What would be the key priorities in the first few months of the job?

What are the company's long term goals?

Where do you see the company in five years time?

What would you say is the most challenging aspect of the role?

What training opportunities does the company offer?

What does the promotional scale look like?

What do you like most about working here?

Do you have any concerns that we can discuss in more detail in order for me to be the top candidate?

When can I expect to hear from you?

Chapter 17

Last But Not Least

Practise

Grab a friend, family member, colleague, your dog…anyone, (ok, maybe not the dog) anyone at all with whom you can practise and receive feedback on both answering and asking questions.

Which questions do you find challenging? Are you normally a smooth talker and certain questions make you stutter or ramble? Practise practise, practise.

If can't find a willing volunteer, try recording yourself. Most mobile phones have a record facility so use this to play back your answers. Do you sound confident, positive and engaging? No? Keep practising until you do.

Good Luck!

So, congratulations for reading to the end of the book. I do hope you found it helpful and are raring to go for your next interview.

Remember by studying and analysing the job description, person specification and researching the company you can second guess which questions you are most likely to be asked.

Create your answers so that they are easily adaptable to meet the variations you may be asked and build your confidence.

It would be great if you got in touch via Twitter or my websites to let me know of any successes you have had.

Good luck!

www.tmscoaching.co.uk

www.facebook.com/tmscoaching

www.linkedin.com/groups/TMS-Coaching-4561002

To follow Jules Halliday

@juleshalliday

Visit my website at www.juleshalliday.com

Coming soon…

The Mystery Shopper Series

Visit my website or follow me on Twitter for regular updates and future titles.

Resources

For a full list and details of all the UK jobsites visit www.allukjobsites.com

For CV writing services or interview practise visit

www.tmscoaching.co.uk

Special Offers

Read on for three special offers to readers of this book.

Special Offer 1

Would you like to practise interview answers?

TMS Coaching offers telephone interview coaching specific to your needs.

Sessions can be booked for an hour, 90 minutes or in blocks for a deeper discount.

The first step is to visit the website www.tmscoaching.co.uk and click on the career coaching tab. You can then choose how many sessions you would like and use our online booking system to select days and times suitable to you.

You will then be emailed a link to fill out a questionnaire which you are advised to fill in and submit back to us with a copy of your CV. This will help us identify your strengths, weaknesses and requirements so we can ask specific questions that you are likely get asked in an interview.

Once completed, we will call you at your chosen appointment time and after a brief introduction, we will conduct the interview and provide verbal, constructive feedback giving you the opportunity to ask any questions.

As a thank you for purchasing this book, we are offering a special discount of 20% off. Just enter the code CVEBOOK at checkout and the discount will be automatically applied.

Special Offer 2

Ok, so you have read the book and feel you now need a bit of help getting reworking your CV? That's ok, we can help.

TMS Coaching offers telephone CV coaching where we provide feedback on your current CV and offer suggestions on changes you should make.

Each session lasts 30 minutes.

The first step is to visit the website www.tmscoaching.co.uk and click on the career coaching tab then select CV Coaching. You can then choose the session you would like from our online booking system to select days and times suitable to you.

You will then be emailed a link asking you to fill out a simple form, upload your current CV and submit back to us we can review it before the call.

Once completed, we will call you at your chosen appointment time and discuss your CV with you.

As a thank you for purchasing this book, we are offering a special discount of 20% off. Just enter the code CVEBOOK at checkout and the discount will be automatically applied.

Special Offer 3

Sometimes job searching can seem like a mammoth task and even a full time job within itself. If you need some direction and expert guidance then check out the three job search packages we have at www.tmscoaching.co.uk on the career coaching section.

As a special offer, we are offering a 20% discount from our Bronze, Silver and Gold packages. Just enter the code CVEBOOK at checkout and the discount will be automatically applied.

Follow TMS Coaching

www.tmscoaching.co.uk

www.twitter.com/tmscoaching

www.facebook.com/tmscoaching

www.linkedin.com/groups/TMS-Coaching-4561002

Follow Jules Halliday

www.juleshalliday.com

www.twitter.com/juleshalliday

www.juleshalliday.hubpages.com

Follow All UK Jobsites

www.allukjobsites.com

www.twitter.com/allukjobsites

Out now and available from Amazon, Lulu & Kobo

CV Creator

Interview Strategies for Success

Coming soon…

The Mystery Shopper Series

Printed in Great Britain
by Amazon.co.uk, Ltd.,
Marston Gate.